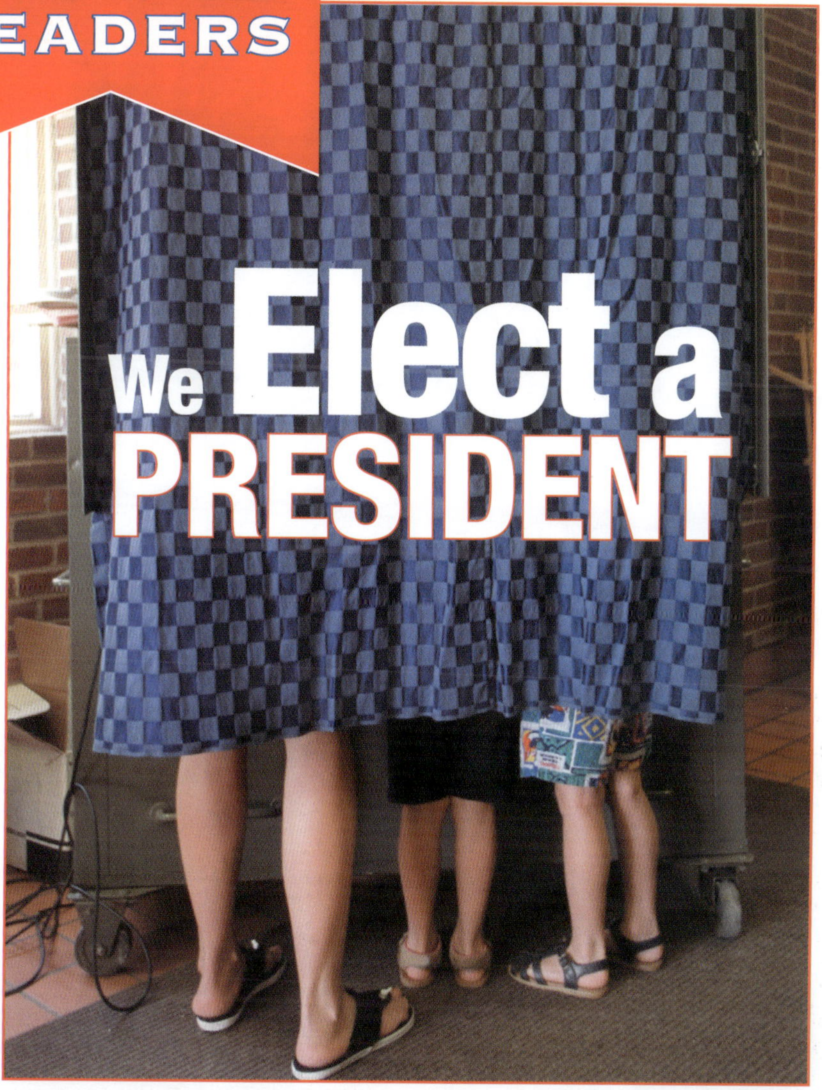

We Elect a PRESIDENT

by Jeri Cipriano

Orlando Austin Chicago New York Toronto London San Diego

Visit *The Learning Site!*
www.harcourtschool.com

SOUTH CAROLINA
W.
W

In the United States, Americans elect a President every four years. To become President, you must have been born a United States citizen. You must have lived in the United States for 14 years or more. You must be at least 35 years old.

Al Gore, a Democrat, ran for President in 2000.

A donkey is the symbol of the Democratic party.

Voters who share the same ideas form groups called parties. The two biggest parties are the Democratic party and the Republican party.

George W. Bush, a Republican, ran for President in 2000.

An elephant is the symbol of the Republican party.

Each party chooses a person to run for President.

The election for President takes place in November. People line up at voting places across the nation to cast their votes. Voters must be citizens of the United States. They must be at least 18 years old.

People wait their turn to vote.

A woman casts her vote by pulling a lever.

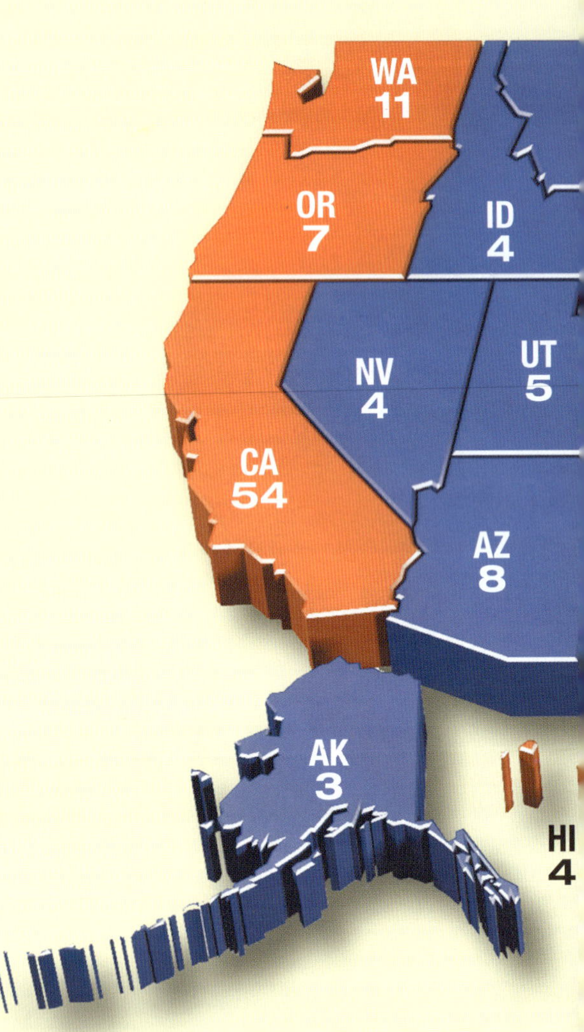

The votes are counted, state by state. The winner of each state gets the electoral votes for that state. The number of electoral votes a state has is based on its population. To become President, a candidate must get 270 of the 538 total electoral votes.

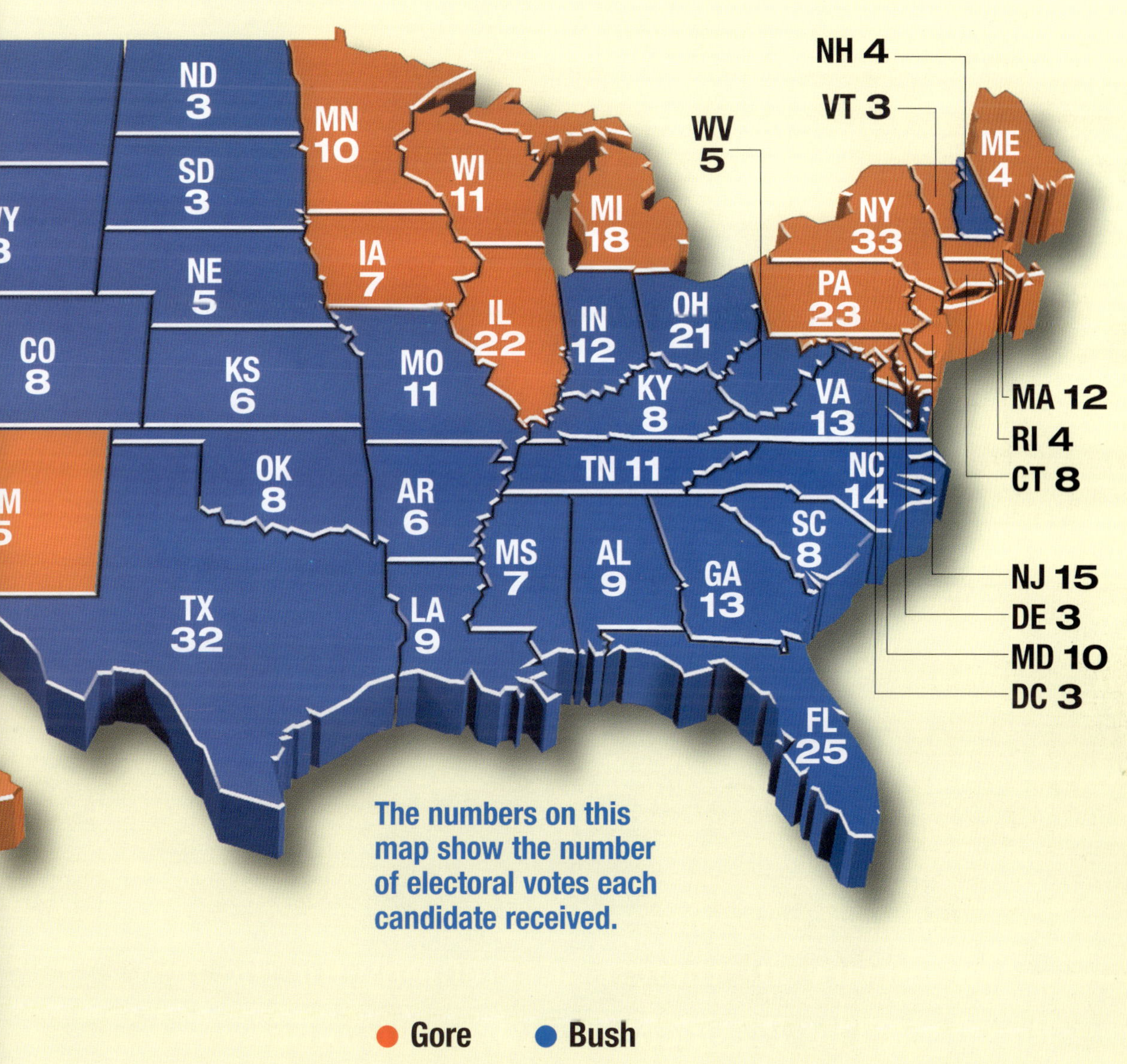

The numbers on this map show the number of electoral votes each candidate received.

President-elect George W. Bush was sworn in as President in January 2001.

On January 20, there is a ceremony for the new President. The President is sworn into office.